BLES CHAVEZ-BERNSTEIN
WITHOUT RHYME

a poet's story

outskirtspress
DENVER, COLORADO

Acknowledgments

For my daughters Yrra and Rehina, my son Eurice, and my husband Steve who have been my most candid and loving critics, and great sources of inspiration; my parents who have supported me unconditionally; the countless family and friends who believed in me, and last but not least, Ma'am Chit, my teacher who saw the "sparkle in my eyes" as a reflection of the world of poetry before I could.

Contents

War Within 1

Oasis for a Child 2

Dance on the Sidewalk 4

Beyond Sandig 6

Fly Us Invisible 8

The Belt 10

The Hammock 11

Old Woman 12

A Song of the Past...14

The Dream House..15

Stranger 16

If I Could Speak to You..17

At Dusk in Paradise 19

Only the Wind Can See..20

The Grass Knows..21

A River Named Grabol...22

Listen to the Walls...24

Pulse 25

What's in a Heart? 26

First Sight...27

I See You Here...28

A Gift of April..29

Wandering..30

Whatever You May Be 31

This Face 32

At the Bus Station 34

Your Silence...36

Where the Path Leads 37

A Different Man..38

Trip to Bittersweet..39

Elegy 40

Not of This World...42

Fatherly Advice...43

Whispers in the Laundry Room 44

At the Long Table 45

One Cold Place...46

Scent of the Enemy 47

The Chair 48
Last Day of Christmas...50
Safe in the Angel's Hands 51
Early Training 53
Nighttime...54
April Love..56
Your Wound...57
Reflections...58
Coming Home..59
Beyond Answers...61
If Forever Waits 62
Desire Unwanted..63
Cyclic Traveler 64
Borrowed Moments..65
Two-way Mirror 66
My Intimate Reminder...67
Malignant Loss...68
Perpetual Dance...70
Caregiver..72
Your Land Smiles at Me 73
How Old I Am 75
The Wrath of Vesuvius 76
Of Pilgrims and Songs 78
At Last..80
There Was a Man 81
Time...82
Through My Window Blinds.....................................83
Overture...85
Raw Dimension..86
The Masters and the Sea..88
Witnesses 90
Perfection...91
Spectrum..92
Brown Beauty...93
A Muted Song 94
Full Circle...95
The Wedding..96
A Singer's Vow 97
The Promise..98
A City in a Fog 100

Old Friends..101
Live Act..102
Uncertainty..103
Behind Those Dreamy Eyes 104
A Woman's Refuge...106
A New Year 107
Regal in Ivory..109
A Girl's Lullaby 110
Somewhere Is Bliss...111
Fireworks...112
This Man I Know 113
Ancient Thread 116
When Truth Becomes Silent....................................118
Butterflies..119
From Here to There 120
Slow Ride to Destiny...122
Stained Glass Windows..123
Sol..124
Shy Moon...126
No Tears to Shed...128
Sands 129
Sound of Laughter..130
Voice of a Poet..131

War Within

The world was perfect
before my three year old eyes.
Crisp laughter ringing,
at times tickling like giggles
all over the bamboo hut,
echoing in the misty valley
where the sun bathes its wings
in mellow gold.
A little infant crawling
with innocent curiosity
while up on his shoulders.
I can see high clouds
painted on her face,
the flowers in her smile
splashing colors over mine.
Today is filled with joy
tucked in our chests
where our hearts commune.
The woman is occupied
but her glances are on us
while she sings music of her daydreams
from a passing youth.
She was born out of love.
He was too, in a war-torn season.

My world was pure and perfect
until the war within began.

Oasis for a Child

This is where I awoke
from an ancient dream,
restless are my thoughts
floating out of a deep well.
They want to fly as high
as the clouds above me.
I was here
before my mother called my name.
The smell of wet grass,
burning rice fields,
carabaos in muddy waters,
fattened piglets,
fowls picking endlessly
on fertile grounds,
brooks murmuring secrets
of the watchful woods,
boldly untamed flowers
telling me tales of long ago.
I take my pail to fill with water
out of a hidden spring.
I speak the language of the birds
whose music is well in tune
with the weather and the moon.
My heart jumps at their chorus,
I get lost in their songs.

Dance on the Sidewalk

A million pair of eyes.
They all look in this direction
but do not see who I am.
I find peace in my hiding,
I love the lights shining
intensely on my face,
following my moves,
chasing shadows away.
Someone has taught me
how to make a sound
from deep within,
to share the language
of a traveling soul.
He props a bench,
I jump on top
to step in stealth
and hop in rhythm.
Percussion is my friend.

The sidewalk stage is transient
so I begin my endless dancing.

Beyond Sandig

A hill peacefully nestled
in a sleeping mountain.
Isarog, a dormant giant
ushering young towns
grow into glittering cities.
Lush and green is her abode
with trees tall as the sky,
heavy rainfall makes curtains
for a show on one life's stage.
Church bells ring at dawn
waking tired, sleepy souls.
Some fish in a moonlit sea,
early risers win money.
The market in the midst of town
boasts of fresh fruits and toys
but not for the children's joy.
Such a rocky and muddy path
where my little feet trod
on an aimless journey.

A million questions in my mind-
beyond hills, trees, and rainfalls
their answers lie.

Soon a child will take a bite
of the endless poetry of life.

Fly Us Invisible

A setting on a dinner table,
a simple serving of food
fit for siblings of busy seven,
the tiniest at the head table
the oldest at the other end.
Hurry everyone, eat and drink,
it's almost six o'clock again!
The clock is ticking away,
hurry everyone, hurry!
I can hear the scary scream
of a raging stranger,
looks unrecognizable,
words loud and too harsh
for our hearts, born soft.
Little eyes still unopened,
unable to face the gust
violently raving.
Run, everyone run!
Let me count the heads here…
Where is everyone?
One's missing, where is she?
Please… go and get her
or she'll get hurt there.

Look everywhere, under covers,
beneath beds, behind doors.
Dinner's gone on the ground,
glasses shattered, plates destroyed.
Table turned upside down,
war-torn dwelling, not a home.

Please… pray and sit still,
wait till this is over.
The night is long and lonely
in a crowd of plenty,
a borrowed home, a refuge
shielding us from the blow
of a nagging nightmare.

Wake us up,
take us back to our dreams
where no one can find us.
Fly us invisible, fly us fast!

The Belt

What are you made of,
remains of animal skin,
were you made to protect
or adorn man's clothing?
Perhaps you're made
of tough intentions,
feeding rage to clenched fists
a noble purpose, they say…
to tame a little child
whose wildness is as pure
as the raindrops in the air.
A traveler in her own world
where fantasies of beauty
are a bountiful reality,
where her hungry spirit
flies high to find its voice.

At last I have found my muse.
I am safe as a recluse.

The Hammock

Up and down I go
drifting in this magical ride,
flowing rhythm, swinging,
my mind deep in a trance.
A few are not in harmony
with my thoughts alive,
creating a chosen path
to a faraway land.

The baby falls asleep
as I sing in her ears
music she would hear
only in her slumber.
I am all alone here
while others beat routines
drawn as a rule
in a house dry and still.
I see brown leaves falling
through a hole in my wall.
The weather is sad,
foreboding of another storm,
a bleak sky is looming
over this empty room.

Wait…
let me sing the last note
of my one unfinished song.

Old Woman

That is how I see her,
short and hunchback,
with glowing brown skin
sunburnt from heavy doses
of the searing *Bicol* sun.
Old and tired
yet wears a constant smile
reserved exclusively
for her loved ones.
Sarong and barong
are her daily fashion,
work is her only treasure.
The only vice she knows
is chewing betel nut and lime.
When seated in a corner
her eyes look far,
she breathes deeply,
calmly savoring
her much deserved prize.
She calls me, "Nisnak!"
A mispronounced "Blesnak".
The missing teeth are no excuse!
I never hear her speak
about her man,
a martyr under the knife
of Japanese hands.
He triumphed over torture
withholding a single word,
offered life a chosen end
for his two guerilla sons.

An unforgettable character
in my early lifeline,
my grandma knew love
as sacred as time.

Lucia Gabriela

A Song of the Past

Do you recall the day
when you said to me,
"Rain will never fall
on a day of summer."?
My heart began to sing
a strange melody
birds came, flowers bloomed...
now everything seems
to be just a memory.
Have you changed your path?
I don't see you,
you don't look my way.
Will I ever hear
summer wind again?

Today is a fading song,
tomorrow is a distant walk.
I hear no other sound
but a hum in the dark.

The Dream House

On rare moments
when I could capture
my father's smile,
our eyes would meet,
our hearts would speak of a vision
shared on common terms.
We'd say, "sliding glass doors
overlooking the garden...",
again and again.
Each time he asked me,
"What is your dream house like?"
over a cup of coffee
and a savored cigarette,
my eager face looked up to his.
Outside the rain was falling hard
on our galvanized roof,
imitating a hundred drums.
Behind the wooden door
was the grass-covered yard .

Years have aged our dream
in the realm of clouds
where my father lives.
Here I am, still waiting
to build the house
with sliding glass doors,
to display the rarest flowers
in a garden he'll never tend.
There's no coffee to savor
nor cigarettes to burn
but he smiles more often now,
with genuine humor and glee
than what I used to see.

Stranger

No one can see light
in this darkened place,
or hear a gurgling brook
in the forest,
pick a rose bud
from its fragile stem
without touching the thorn.
No one can ease the pain
of a man in his sickbed,
tired and beaten
from decades of toil.
Was it by chance
that I lost my lot to choose
when a voice called my name?

Inside my home
lives a quiet stranger.

If I Could Speak to You

Souls behind *labourean* walls,
listen to my quivering voice,
I'm here outside, alone and cold.

T'was not too long ago
when your gates with open arms
embraced my helpless wonder.
Your *nipa* shed sheltered me
from the pouring rains
that never washed away
images of your loving reign.
The little bridge too often
took my steps to a pond
behind the creaking bamboos,
a perfect mirror
for silent wings of a naïve dreamer.
Morning rush in a bus,
the dormant *Mt Isarog* smiled
as she witnessed my sleepy rides.
I used to run to fall in line,
sing along at the morning ritual,
too many questions
to satisfy my virgin mind.

Amidst tears and laughter,
drama, books, and numbers,
I raced to reach my goals.
Suddenly a distant call
echoed the last page of our play.
I heard so many footsteps
behind the deserted stage
yet no one was there but me.
I know I have sung a few lines
of a song yet unwritten
as curtains fell before the crowd.

If I could speak to you
I would tell of the roads
I've crossed and left behind,
with you who has paved paths
for life to blossom
as hesitant buds decide to bloom .

At Dusk in Paradise

The mighty light of heaven from its throne descends,
weary petals break away from their stems
while the bird finds its home in a tree,
the farmer's suit stiffens with the drying mud.

The heavenly arc does not turn fully dark
when one is waiting for his destined time
while crimson pours over the grayish sky
the poet finds the restless music of the rhyme.

But what else is there that a man desires
if he possesses wealth, love, and power?
Is it honor, fame, glory altogether?
Perhaps unknown is why he hungers.

There is but one way to paradise
but man's losses blur its way.
The innocence of a child,
the white velvet of the lily,
and an inner treasure to pave his journey.

Oh, man! If you can't master your earthly strife,
why not seek the hidden beauty of life?

Only the Wind Can See

Only the wind could see
the curtains I peeped through
when some familiar shadow
passed by my window.
It caught my lazy gaze
at the moist grass
on that humid afternoon.
It heard my thoughts
as I chased your hurried steps
on a night when a lonely leaf
hanging loosely on a twig,
refused to see the naked moon.
When the moment was not on time
and the cold wrapped the sick
I almost choked in your frozen grip.

Now here in my home
the gardenia, fertile and warm,
still longs for the mist of dawn.
Desiring silently, waiting restlessly
but only the wind can see.

The Grass Knows

Even the grass knows
long after they've withered
that I've run my fingers through
green leaves of a certain fall.
I stumbled upon a pebble
rolling swiftly on a grassy path
where footsteps are faded
by storms and wild wind
of a recent past.

The trees are bare now
but still standing tall
in the depth of the woods
where silent dreams are heard
from a spirit born to soar.

A River Named Grabol

In my little town under the bridge
she keeps a low profile,
almost invisible
as she quietly rides.
She is a child of the waterfalls
from the olden woods.
She's shallow in summer
but deep in September.
Witness to many tales
of woes and laughter,
she eagerly listens
to whispers of honeyed lips
at secret encounters
of scared young lovers.
She sounds angered after a storm,
the soothing calmness
in her graceful stream
turns into a raging flowage.
She almost caught the girl
with the saddest eyes
but someone held her back
from jumping to the bed of rocks,
when the world crumbled
in her dimmed horizon.

The river flows and flows
with no remorse for the afflicted
nor celebration for success.
She does as she's told by her gods,
"You have one purpose and only one…
to flow until you're dry.
Your water will feed all who chooses life."

Listen to the Walls

They start whispering low
when I play with the night
as faces kiss the pillows
and stars go out of sight.
They see me crawl upstairs
as darkness swallows day,
pages of books unread,
untouched by hands
wanting to pluck strings instead!
By the time I say, "Good morning."
friends have done it an hour before,
never the first to awake
as I'm the last to yawn.
I much regret that one morning
no one has seen me rise
faster than the pastel dawn!
I never seem to be
where everyone is.
Am I out of rhythm
with everybody's beat?
Perhaps there's a different drum
beneath my dancing feet.

Pulse

I look for your face in the crowd
I hear loud whispers,
quiet breathing,
your eager hand slipping into mine.
I trace the lines that frame
the most loved face,
playful lips speaking
of a promised bliss.
Behind the door that conceals
signs and motions
revealing our window talks,
awkward conversations,
the balcony holds your silhouette
as I, the pulse of your naked heart.

What's in a Heart?

What lies inside...
is it blood spurting,
love burning?
Is it divine beauty,
a rarity to behold?
Is it a pump
to feed romance,
a hollow chamber
drawing other hearts
to fill empty spaces
with nothing but desire?
What makes it whole
or less,
perhaps its nature
is to find in us
our own completeness.

First Sight

In the midst of a noisy hall
there was you standing alone.
Suddenly the room felt empty,
your eyes were magnets
drawing mine to see nothing
but your presence
imposing, electrifying
and I, for the first time,
became an obedient follower.
I spoke with no voice,
my lips found no words,
my steps unmoved.
Seconds… minutes…
time stood and waited
but I did nothing
but fall in love.

I See You Here

What shall I count-
seconds, minutes, hours?
Something haunts my thoughts,
thoughts devour my time.
I still hear
the echo of your laughter
resounding through the rain
as you crossed the busy streets
holding me suspended
in that moment,
unmoving,
cars beeping loud like sirens
but I wasn't listening.

Our eyes meet
through many shadows.
It is first sight again.

A Gift of April

Like a wisp of air
blowing softly on my skin,
a faint caress,
a plea for my name.
You called me
when you needed another soul
to talk to not with words
but with looks
that would find me melting
at the fire of your touch.
Who are you?
Tucked in a box,
hidden in layers
of mysterious wrapping
covering your thoughts,
your dreams kept
in an almost forgotten sleep.
Peeling each thin covering
reveals a diamond
smiling at an envious sky,
leaving me undressing,
naked and alive.

Wandering

This February breeze
brings nostalgia to my soul
as it wanders in the meadow
not far from my beloved sea.
Through a shattered window
I see your face fading
among the reddened clouds
slowly turning gray
to bid us a cold goodbye.
My heart freezes
as I'm thrown into an icy lake,
loneliness swims deep in the waters,
my senses no longer wake.

There's a place beyond this earth
where time does not exist.
When daylight shines again
I vow to meet you there.

Whatever You May Be

When you become a sturdy tree
shadowing a virgin meadow,
I become the leaves sprouting
as you magically grow.
…an arrogant skyscraper
playing with the sun,
or the ocean caressing the earth,
I become the ripples running
to the edge of the waters.
When you're a child on helpless feet
discovering the hurt of a sudden fall,
something in me wants to run
to hold you as you rise.

How much time must I spend,
how much love must I give?

If only time can measure love…

This Face

Who is this little child
lying next to me?
I see your tiny face,
the look of porcelain,
the touch of silk,
flawless as the dawn
with its nurturing glow
on a new, pale sky.
I am drawn to you,
you are part of me.
Little hands and feet
helpless and delicate,
eager, hungry mouth
seeking warmth from my chest
motherhood fulfilled…
life sustained,
nature wills.
A soul full of beauty,
took form out of love,
a mirror of the future,
my first glimpse of a miracle!

At the Bus Station

Your eyes are simply asking
why mommy has a suitcase
too heavy for my hands,
my grip weakened,
my strides slowed down
by the weight of my heart.
It is laden with grief
at the loss of time
to hold you in my arms
in the quiet of nights,
when you cry, begging
for a motherly cuddle,
food from my breasts,
touch of my hand,
and certainty of love.
Now I want to leave
all alone by myself
so I can pretend
I'm not saying goodbye
to my little girl
in the arms of the woman
whose spirit is kind to me.
My instincts are pulled apart
as my heart is being torn,
pumping tears and blood
for a fate unknown.

Sacrifice paints color
on this one face of love.

Your Silence

Your silence is like a knife
piercing, hurting.
Oh, how it turns my heart
so quiet and still.
Dreams around me
seem to look too far.
My eyes start to well
for the tears on their way.

If I can't stand the cold
can I feel the warmth
that has yet to unfold
beneath your smile?
When in time I break away
from your wordless spell
I'd let love burn me
so my smoke can fly
to find heaven beyond hell.

Where the Path Leads

I hear the murmur of the night
behind the trembling leaves.
For years it has been silent,
no words, no songs
until you came.

Then my world changed,
took on another shape.
Now the moon whispers
and lights up dark corners
in my chosen road.
If beauty has power
then magic is in every flower.
Yet beauty falls short of meaning
in my quest to quench my thirst
and calm my restless longing.
I walk on a long path
with the hope to meet you
but hope wants to die.
In the dark blue ocean
I swim to its farthest end
where the waves break in ripples,
and its mouth kisses heaven.

I will find you there.

A Different Man

What has become of you?
I often ask myself
a question never answered.
Entranced by your charm
I followed you.
There was magic in your arms
when they held my body tight
in an embrace,
we become bonded in warmth
that changed our worlds.

Beyond the horizon
there is you.
Distance cannot blur
the lines of your face,
the curve of your mouth.
In your eyes is a child
with endless faith
in life's promises.
I see a man transformed
by the smile of a baby girl,
helpless as a bud.

A boy has become your shadow,
his dad is his god.
Beautiful miracles borne
out of fervent devotion
to a lifetime vow
from a man who has become
a father and mother
in one true love.

Trip to Bittersweet

Two adults, two toddlers
trailing on the walkway,
set on a long, tedious ride
above clouds in dark and light.
Beyond the stormy dusk
they fly ahead of time,
bodies weakened by goodbyes
to familiar hugs and lullabies.
Where are you going, stranger?
Are you looking for a place
with distant chances?
The old home has gone too small
for dreams dreamt long ago.
The boy is quiet and follows you,
the little girl is sickened
by everything new.
Before her eyes
looms monstrous strangeness
too scary to tell about.
Her scream drowns the engine sound
but fades when everyone awakens
to the swaying palms
and the warmth of salty breeze.

Elegy

Should I speak of your dying
when how you lived
is what I remember?
You'll never be a memory
as your body rejoins earth.
I rejoice over the truth of your peace
but why am I crying?
My face feels the gentle kisses
you failed to give except for few.
I tried some baby talk
but you took me as wise and grown.
The puzzled child in me
resented seeds of courage
disguised as coldness,
fatherly wisdom unknown.
I used to hide my tears
when you left my pathways rough,
paving future moments
for life's eternal strife.
I longed for sweet caresses,
fatherly cuddles, childish whims.
You stored them all away
in a box of wishes,
gave nothing more
but rules and dreams.
As my heart grieves in silence
I hear you speak again.
I don't feel alone now
as my journey begins.
In the smile of every sunrise,
I am glared by your brilliance.
With every thorn in my skin
I learn your strength again.
As I run fast and stumble,
your perseverance is my goal.

For every flicker of doubt
on a moonless night,
your wisdom is my sight.

The legacy of you
I see in my child's eyes.

Not of This World

You're the face of an angel,
that is your name.
Your soul is old,
sharing thoughts
of rare wisdom.
Kind and calm
in the face of chaos,
distractions in a house
filled with noise.
You touch the keys
with innocent passion
like you always knew
every sound it holds.
Your fingers move
to create music
you always held
deep inside of you.
Who is your teacher?
How do you know?
You simply say,
"I hear it in my head."
You transform sounds
into a magical chorus
sung by a thousand spirits,
serenading us with voices
unheard before,
flying our senses
in suspended exhilaration.

We hear your love
as we open our hearts.
We see your beauty
as we close our eyes.

Fatherly Advice

Ironing a pile of wrinkled shirts,
a normal household scene,
typical and quite moving,
a man's sincere attempt
at practical romancing.
Here comes his three-year old,
preoccupied with her business
of play and girlish trinkets.
He stops her for a second
to speak with manly wisdom,
"You must learn this early on."
But to his dismay
he hears her loud and clear,
"I won't have to, daddy."
Surprised and eager to hear
her inner thoughts
on the subject matter,
he asked the girl in pink,
"Who do you think will do it then?"
With doubtless confidence
she quickly retorts,
"My husband will."

Whispers in the Laundry Room

Baskets filled to the brim,
piles of clothes
touching the ceiling.
Here I am, find me,
I'm not hiding intentionally.
There's little room
for the two of us.
What a cozy break
from the usual runs!
It's quiet here
except for the motor drill,
no one can see us
but the slick chameleons.
Would you bring close to my face
old sweet nothings
meant for my ears alone
just like old times
when you took me to the dance?
I heard your whispers
drown the sound
of the four-man band.

At the Long Table

Weak and fatigued
from a lingering flu,
I push my body
for a tiny bite of pizza
with the happy three.
Everyone's pleased,
conversations welcomed.
The youngest is the first to sit,
the second girl comes next
running away from the boy
who's incessantly crying
for losing a gun-filled fantasy
after she wakes him up
to a blunt reality …
she's done with the game.
"Why can't I have a brother?!"
I snap,
"Why don't you tell your dad."
I hold my breath
to hide the grin behind my face.
"Would he say yes?"
Again I snap,
"Why don't you ask your dad!"
"What if he no longer has…
those tiny stuff I've read about?"
He grabbed an encyclopedia,
to show a picturesque page-
R for reproduction revealed!
The boy keeps nagging,
beaten and frustrated,
tears running down his cheeks.

A laughable moment
at the old, long table.
The boy's grown now,
still waiting for the brother
who never came.

One Cold Place

A red van running through
yellow blinking lights,
student vests showcase faces
with unfinished dreams
left behind by a shallow sleep
from a tired, shadowed night.
Hurried steps on busy streets
take men to their fateful places.
Ours bring us to a nearby stop,
a temporary shelter for our hopes.
Healing hands, printed words,
formulas to kill the incurable ,
most elusive, the unknown,
but it's nowhere to be found.
Children lost in a grown-up world,
how deep our wounds have gone,
yet no one can see
the terror lurking behind
like a thief aiming at his prey.
The enemy is almost winning
as we embrace each other
with prayers drenched in tears.

The boy stays inside his thoughts,
the girl's arm finds a resting place
on her sister's shoulders,
our thoughts speak to each other.
Why spend time in this cold place?
There's no one here but strangers
intruding in our sacred ground
where fun was once the daily rule
and laughter filled the sound .
Our smiles are losing their glow
as we stop the tick of time.

Hope lingers in this one cold place.

Scent of the Enemy

Beds aligned in perfect rows,
you're one among the many,
same as the rest of them.
Not to us… you're the only one,
the force that binds the circle,
the unbroken thread
that guards our home.
We're murmuring pleasantries
with those dressed in white-
expert opinions, medical advice,
dispersed discussions about infusions
never intended to cure.
But just in case…
there's a miracle in science,
in your body or in the mixture
where stubborn cells are winning
the game of mystery,
while you keep drifting
to a place unknown,
you keep flying back and forth
to a space distant from us,
your loves, your life!

Where have you been,
Where are you going?
Why now,
won't you take us with you?
Don't you leave us here!
I smell the scent again,
It is here among us, is it now?

The Chair

It's a simple chair with corduroy flair,
your soft and warm companion
on many sleepless nights.
It carries your lightness,
faithful to your wishes,
a witness to your sadness,
weakening hope, and grief.
It feels the loving affection
from dad's girls playing
with their scrabble wits,
holding a spoon to your mouth
feeding you like a baby,
as you feign appetite
to bring out their smiles.
It stands the fearful look in your son
when he walks away from your glance.
The chair sends an invitation
for everyone to sit on its lap,
as it feels the weight of sorrow
borne by the heart of each guest.
It has but one thing to give -
soft reassurance of warmth,
a passing ease of suffering
for a tired and breathless man.

So everyone can rest from their toil
the chair always waits in the corner.

Last Day of Christmas

Brilliant colors blinking
red, white, gold, and silver
the children are in awe!
We bring them here
to a place of merriment,
giving them a little rest
from the silent terror
of losing your presence,
a mystery to them.
Your eyes are happy
without the glow,
content is your smile
without excitement.
I hide a heavy load inside
so no one would ever know
that here, it is empty and dark .
The choir sings grandiosely
on a skyline stage.
Angels are looking over us,
watching our every footstep
lest it loses its way to home.

Safe in the Angel's Hands

Today seems like any other day,
a warm modest kitchen
smelling of spicy scents,
a weak attempt to please
a bland palate, a fragile body
of once a stoic figure,
vibrant soul with dry humor
that used to stir laughter
and endless smiles
in anyone who drifted by.

Today is like any other day,
children ramming the door
after a long drill in school,
but unlike any other day,
they kiss his cold cheeks
fear caught in their eyes,
shivers in their spines
as he makes grueling noise
drilling deeply into our beings,
telling us without words
of ominous signs.

We are too blinded by love,
death is as foreign as life
for youth has just begun.
His spirit, strong as the storm
looming over our home
but his body's weakened
by a treacherous enemy .
Medicines have lost power,
my vision blurred by fear.

Let us hold you one more time,
feel you in this dimension,
I forgot how love began.

To the young I whispered,
"We will be safe in the angel's hands."

Early Training

A tiny ball made of foam,
a tiny plastic basket
on the living room wall.
Little did anyone know
They would soon become
sentimental mementos
for a girl who holds a star
in the basketball court.
Precision is her gift
when tossing the ball
in an upward swoop!
Dribbling, passing,
running, docking,
she becomes invisible
as speed hides her
from fierce opponents.
Once lithe and short,
nicknamed "shrimp"
by her little friends,
her statuesque elegance
bears a vengeful humor!
It's not just the Jersey shirt
with printed numbers,
nor the graceful movement
of her supple limbs,
or the sight of her slim figure
flying in the air.
There's something more
constant within her.
The passion and love
for the game she plays
is a precious legacy of a man,
the coach she does not see.

Nighttime

Dark, quiet hours, where are you?
You know when I need you.
Everyone is asleep now,
children lost in their dreams,
resting from the glare of day
and nagging faces of strangers.
Too many questions asked,
they always fall on barren ears
unwelcomed, unanswered.
The absence of sound
becomes my closest friend
when my voice inside
screams the loudest.
My cry fades among the dust
as my tears run dry
and sadness numbs my mind.

When you closed your eyes,
I did not mean to say goodbye.

April Love

A photograph of a woman's face
tells tales of a sweet affair,
young love of a distant past
coming in to my present.
Seeing your face closely
sets the story's ending.
You return to a time
that takes you to my home.
You look at my children
searching for his smile,
don't you see him alive
in their eyes?
You bring carnations to his grave
that would soon fade,
they're ephemeral as the clouds
unlike his promise.
We're warmed in his embrace
where we'll always find
what his love bequeaths .

Your Wound

You bear the face of my son
but I miss the voice
calling me, "mom".
Your silence is not cold,
it burns our hearts.
I still see you running
to look for the place
where dad was taken.
Is your grief overflowing
from deep inside
that there's no more room
for our affection?
Your eyes scream
the look of tearful rage!
Your quiet anger bears a dagger
piercing through our bones.
Please tell us, look our way.
Pain is not your friend.
if I could touch it,
I would take it from you,
or beg it to go away.
We miss your playful spirit
warming our home,
creating vibrant sounds
along the walls.
Let us touch you once again
so our wounds will fade
and yours can heal,
Dad never left, he's here.

Reflections

In darkness you may not see
who you are,
your brightness,
your desire.
When everything shatters
you struggle to stay sane.
You may not know
who you really are,
your spark,
your beauty,
and your desire
until you start seeing
your own reflections
in my eyes,
in my being,
then you start believing.

In the light of love.

Coming Home

A sudden sniff of scent
piercing my senses,
sketching my thoughts...
takes me back to a place
too familiar to ignore.
A pair of little hands
gripping my hem,
six little feet eager to run
on a grassy path
browned and burned
by the breath of summer.
Gardenias in bloom
with its glare of white
tell us to start our ritual
of coming home.

The aroma of rice steaming
permeates the modest kitchen,
ambiance of heartwarming refuge
for a hungry crowd.
Playful hands and feet,
endless laughter and tease,
eyes full of innocence
and unsuspecting fears
kissed away by a man
in the comfort of my presence.

Lost amidst the dutiful routine,
I create a world away
in search for my truth.

As I open my eyes again,
the little hands and feet
are no longer there
in this cozy home
that has felt every touch,
and has heard every breath
we have shared.

In a cold corner frozen by time,
the sagging chair is empty
but the loving man opens the door
each time we come home.

Beyond Answers

Wordless I'm drawn
to wander in a time
far and unknown
yet feels forever.
Have we met before
in a place forgotten
where warm desires
can blur our sight?
Does fate intend to play
with our burning hearts,
will tranquility stay
in the midst of reason?
Should I answer your call
as it draws my spirit
to walk this long road
until dawn turns to dusk?

I see reflections of my own
in the depth of your eyes,
fueled by passion,
silenced by love.

If Forever Waits

I would begin to think of you
much less than always
only if I know
how long forever waits.
Spring would starve for color
less reminding of your warmth,
your touch with lukewarm ardor
as you lose me in your arms.
The sun's heat would be subtle,
the moon would be hiding
as I await your call
and whisper my loudest cry.
Longing would never be
as sad as my tears,
the ones you failed to see
as my fears fade away.
With a timid kiss
barely touching your lips
I will secretly yearn for you
with reluctant passion.
Time I would steal
to give my love rest
for one moment…
but only if forever waits.

Desire Unwanted

The first time we met
my fate took a turn
as I touched you,
held you.
My body shivered
at the bolt of joy!
My heart leaped
as my mind froze
in ecstasy.
I kiss you every day,
breathe your scent
constantly.
Drunk from the drops
of nectar oozing
from your soul,
I weep and laugh
not seeing my path
anymore.
Why has my beloved rose
stopped blooming
from its bush?
I see its petals fall,
brown on the edges,
leaves crackling
as they crumble
under strangers' steps.
Even as happiness
comes to me
as a faceless promise,
I still desire you
with a poisonous want,
until I make my final bow
… of surrender.

Cyclic Traveler

I see you come and go.
I watch you pause…
at a stop where we meet
every time you need
a dose of human contact.

Do you see me?

Finding a way to your world
brings a soothing hope
that you can believe in something.

Please believe.
I have.

Borrowed Moments

You bless me
with glimpses of a past life
when you were younger
with silken skin
flawless,
glowing,
under any shade of light.

In silence you hand me
a photo that remembers
a thousand images
suspended in rapid movements
of fashion, color, laughter,
and pretense.

With fickle bursts of insights
your spirit joins me
giggling over stories
of youth from long ago.

Aaah! the sound of sudden screams
awakens us out of our dream.

Two-way Mirror

Every time I speak to you
you see my lips move
but you don't hear the words.

When I touch you,
don't you feel
the faint knock I make
on the door
of your hollow heart?

If I find meaning
in your loss
I might find the bridge
from suffering to ease.

I might see my face
looking through
a two-way mirror.

My Intimate Reminder

In a familiar hallway
our steps often meet,
I look into your eyes
and see a world far away.

Is it pain that you defy,
the random creation
of confusing stimuli,
a genetic error,
one flaw of nature?

Here I am, humbled.
I offer my hand
to touch your distant soul.
My intentions seem to fail,
your pain prevails.

I murmur thoughtless words
as you make me laugh. Cry.
I cling to my loves - my life!

Across the familiar hallway
my steps are freer.

My comrade.
My intimate reminder.

Malignant Loss

Pain has become his aura,
his world has shrunk
to the size of his bed.
His legs, once powerful,
ran the winning score
before the raving crowd.
Now they are nothing
but a mass of skin
hiding a skeletal frame.

It was always his will,
wild and untamed,
that made him lose
the one life's bet,
a gamble played.

It's too late now
to stop the countdown.
He bargains, he pleads
but can't say a word.
He touches his back
where the stubborn wound
has found a home.
A lonely grimace fills his face
telling a tale of agony.

Beyond his reach
is another wound
more vicious than the first.
It blew away from his eyes,
the last flicker of smile
after his love left him
a thousand times
before Goodbye.

Perpetual Dance

As long as I remain
to this aged planet,
a loyal friend,
my body will always feed
on its water and air.
I rest and sleep
to replenish my strength
then I awake in time
when the night is gone
to do them again.

My consciousness
bears sole witness
to the mysteries
of our passing strife.
But when I dance
I soar to distant heights,
to a hidden place
that belongs to no one.
My body breathes
to lift my arms,
my limbs,
my hands.
They all move in rhythm
as perfectly as my desires.
My hips sway as I twist to find
the elegance and grace
only heaven can define.
As music guides
the tempo of my pulse,
dance raises my soul,
feeds my every bone,
for every dream inside.

Caregiver

My hands are always free
when you need them
to set the clock of care,
a meticulous regimen.
My arms are here
reaching out to warm you
in your cold bed
set in a ward full of suffering.
I am the only voice you hear,
the only face you see,
I am by your side
when loved ones are distant.
Moans, groans,
painful screams,
acts of struggle and fighting
for a life made fragile
by a mortal system.
I am an instrument
of healing and comfort,
a narrow bridge
between ill and well.
My touch brings magic
as it feels your skin,
I relieve your pain.
I am a servant of the spirit
that loves all men,
despite what humans do
to alter earthly harmony
creating needless chaos
in a world full of beauty
and unseen destiny.

I was born rich
so I can give.
I am your caregiver.

Your Land Smiles at Me

Walking through the crowded *soi*,
vendors of food and more,
I look like I'm one of you
wearing your complexion,
I smile often too.
When I speak your native tongue
I hit and miss but I survive.
The laugh I keep to myself,
you're forgiving of my accent.
The aroma of sticky rice,
grilled gizzards,
soup and spice,
seduce my palate to indulge,
an exotic feast galore!
On the streets and every alley
is a market full of wealth-
shoe repair, dressmakers,
salons for nails and hair,
the most pleasing of them all-
a masseuse on every corner.
Gifted hands,
soothe my achy feet,
uptight shoulders,
neck, and head.
Oh heal my body, please!
Nirvana is this place.
A secret haven,
a heaven filled
with brown-skinned women
their figures petite and thin,
in frozen awe men are smitten.
They seem to always please,
meet everyone's needs,
spoiling pampering they give.
Your smile is sweeter
than the spoken word,

for I have yet to learn
your ancient language,
you have yet to know my own.
This is my newfound home
where temples are adorned,
churches are not doomed.
Prayers are sacred here
and so is penitence
just like what I have learned
from teachers and elders.

Your land smiles endlessly,
the Buddha welcomes me.

How Old I Am

Brick roads surviving
centuries of fests and wars,
witnessing man's story
unchanging .
Giant statues hovering,
making statements
on lifestyles past.
Kings, queens, and soldiers
clad in pompous elegance.
Angels and martyrs,
deceased popes and saints,
their relics secured
in basilicas and cathedrals.
My ancestors could have been
among your servants,
royal concubines,
illegitimate sons
or daughters of kings.
I could have come
from a blue bloodline...
but what color paints a soul?
Ponte Vecchio ,
I cross your bridge
to pass the old river,
witness to countless rides.
By the *Trevi* fountain
I wish for the greatest love
and toss my little coin.
"No, young man,
don't sell me flowers."
Let me stay in this dream,
let me fly back to a time
when my name was different,
maybe then I'll understand
why I am here.

The Wrath of Vesuvius

A visit made,
a homage paid.
What does it serve your souls
that have gone to a time
forgotten by the living?
Here I am stepping
on your holy ground,
a city of beauty
built by skillful hands,
homes covered in stucco
designed with the artist's tools.
For centuries
you have watched your children
play and run the vast landscape
spread below your heights.
What sparked your anger,
sudden outburst,
was it too much indulgence
in merriment and joy?
Did this puppy deserve
to be clad in cast
while he gasped for air,
or this man,
as he ran with his child
to some place hidden
from your flames?
No blood splattered nor seen,
you chose to conceal the horror
inside cemented bodies,
muting their screams
while breathing took its end.
Your smoke of death
has buried many dreams,
your memories have left us
nothing but sketches
of the artist's daring vision
of the future earth.

Bones and remains
of the indulgent
give us glimpses
of what could have been,
the grandeur,
the glory,
the happiness
that was etched only
in these ruins of memory.

Of Pilgrims and Songs

For a moment I thought
I left my old companion
when my last travel took me
to an abode adorned
with fragrant orchids,
steep rooftops,
abundant gold.

I stayed alone in my corner
unsure of my song
until a warm breeze
swiftly carried me afloat.

I feel safe.
Unafraid of the cold.

Faces greet me, faces go.
They must be traveling too.
Days pass, faces change
as I learn their songs
and listen to their tunes.

My steps turn into dance!
My songs turn into hymns
and silent chants.
I murmur ardent prayers
that turn into a gentle whisper

Of love.

Lucie Gabrieli

At Last

Home is coming back
to sounds and colors
too entrancing to resist.
A lifestyle expressed
in an artful dance,
long skirts of intricate design
only skillful hands could bear,
if only to feed these eyes
that hunger for beauty.
Words filled with sentiments
from a childhood's past,
spoken in my native tongue.
A language of passion,
lifeline for my spirit.

There Was a Man

With a strong grasp
he held my little hands,
gently guided my steps
along the road long and rough,
until I found my home.
With humor he dropped surprises,
in a crowd he stirred some laughs ,
a few sentimental treats
to make kids smile,
I wanted to emulate his style.
At a distance he was hovering
like a vast pair of wings,
he had us covered
from thunder and wind.
In times of calm
he was a whisper of affection,
a gentle reminder
that he was in me and I in him .

There is a man who is closer
than the air I breathe.
His name was Steve…
but I call him "Father".

Time

Warm smiles greet me
in the wake of the morning
I tap the keys...
work begins.

The ticking hands keep on
telling me nothing
but a hint of time.

I seek time but find none.

Through My Window Blinds

The spots are all aligned,
bordered in white,
inviting each guest
to take brisk steps
to the opened door.
They wait in line
as their faces tell
unwritten plots of countless tales.

The glassy texture of the waters
flowing by the patio
illuminates well
the lacquered piano.
As the keys sing
with each caress
of passionate fingers,
I bathe my day
in the sweltering sky!
At night,
I drink the essence of the moon.

But wait…
there's one more window
apart from all the rest
where blinds stay open,
where light is glaring
and almost blinding
from too much life!

I thrive on you,
my one old love,
my faithful guardian.
Your brilliance glows
with sparkling hues
scattered in my horizon,
a lifelong dream defined .

Again I peek
through my window blinds,
outside it's black
when it is nighttime.

Overture

Long ago I was told
by someone whose voice
was wise and old,
that so much lies
beyond my eyes.
I wondered then
what could I not see
behind the bleakish gray.

Years flashed.
My vision changed.

I have taught my heart
how to listen
to the sound
of an overture playing
to the music's end.

Eagerly I listened
again...and again.

The music is never still.

Raw Dimension

Wandering eyes
set on a pretty face,
you must not see who I am
as you throw your moves away.
Fluid and masterful,
I wonder where your heart is
when you dance.
Agile and wild,
climbing the tallest branch,
flying like a bird
but without wings
to carry you...lest you fall.
You stir primitive impulses,
raw in their fantasies
as each soul in the crowd
gets caught in a trance.

The Masters and the Sea

The stage is full and noisy
as strings are plucked
by virtuoso hands,
unrestrained beats
of the booming drums
drown the timid bass
in the middle of the band.

Johnny Cash sings again
through strained voices,
as they rock and roll like Elvis.
Children twirl, women dance!
Tattoos on their sunburnt skin
are unwillingly displayed
when skirts are fondly lifted
as eager feet step in tempo
on the sandy dance floor.

Nearby, the sea goes on
sending its waves roaring,
kissing the thirsty shores
in harmonious rhythm
with the children's laughter.
Music plays like the old days
as the faces of the masters
become living canvasses
bearing stories of youth
I will never see.

Alone, the sea dances
as the last note rings
from the masters' stage.

Witnesses

They appear from everywhere,
I see faces that remember
our times in years past
when we were beset
with worries and wonderment,
pursuits and sacrifices.
Laughter comes back in a flash
as we see in each other's eyes
our never-changing youth.

Perfection

Once in a while
there is perfection:
a pink skyline
from an early sunburst.
At dusk,
a giant moonrise
sprinkles diamond lights
on the waterways...
for a second
I am floating in space!
I see the blue
of an endless dome,
glistening in golden hues,
the sun glorifies space,
priceless for its worth.
The same sun descends
with its rays
splattered over my city
in glorious crimson.

A humbling vision.

Spectrum

Beams of colors
in precise array
of distinct hues,
artfully paints the sky
as I gaze in awe.
Hazy as a dream,
a magical whim .
Desires long to unfold
when rain clouds appear,
it's been a lifelong chase
to reach your misty end.

If you look closely
in my eyes you'll see
a rainbow smiling.

Brown Beauty

Is this the look of love?
Brown eyes and a childish smile
meant only for my senses,
one moment among a few.

Too precious to touch
with my mortal hand,
I savor it from a distance
lest it vanishes into oblivion...

A Muted Song

I swim in an ocean
that is dry and thirsting
for a few droplets
from the living air.
The child still dances
to the beat
of wants
and dreams…
yet my lips, unmoved,
my tongue presses
against the silence
of my voice.

No one hears what I sing
for the music written
has a muted sound.

Full Circle

A narrow path coils
in the center of the woods
leading my little feet.
Ahead there is mist
that moves along in my direction
veiling the palms in whitish lace.

I pass by a frozen pond
bearing my reflection
with my child's smile.
Suddenly time rushes
to heal my blinded sight.
Time is my friend
when sadness lingers,
a cold stranger when I laugh.
Now I see...
the child is no longer mine.

The Wedding

A faint breeze
greets the red carpet
with a solemn kiss
as the bride lights up
in her ivory gown,
a soft tulle veiling her face
reveals impressionistic art.
Walking down the aisle with her
keeps my feet off the ground.
Canon in D playing on the organ,
light bursting
through stained glass walls,
teary-eyed smiles sharing our joy...
where did these moments go?

Singing "The Voice of My Beloved",
leads me to my child's home...
old photos of a girl on her dad's lap,
with her brother and sister,
in her little tutu,
a little girl standing tall
next to a grand piano
when she was five...
where have these moments gone?

In the midst of white roses,
orchids, and lilies,
our dance in slowed motion
turns into a muted conversation
between us.
She cries...
but her tear drops
with the sound of love
and not goodbye.

A Singer's Vow

Humming, singing
note after note,
shaping the tune,
sculpting the music,
slow and purposeful,
disciplined in rigor,
details and all.
Lyrics next,
then every word,
shaping the lips,
masking the face,
living on stage
as someone else.
One moment
she's in heaven,
next she is in hell!

As the singer
breathes life into her song
the listener transforms.

The Promise

In a valley shadowed
by a sleeping mountain,
lies a town in the midst of smoky hills,
home to a child of a recurring past.
A dialect etched in my tongue
warming the edges of my lips
as it tells the story of a girl
eager to live her life...
she ran so fast
she left her heart behind.

In her heart is a buried promise
that one day she will return -
to play in the narrow streets
leading to the lonely *nipa* hut,
soak her dress in the tropical rains,
wade in the aging river
thirsting for hidden waterfalls,
walk barefoot in the churchyard
as she fills her hometown
with the music of her hymn.

A City in a Fog

I hop in and out of cable cars,
browsing through designs of edifices
on the old streets.
I pay homage to fine pieces of art
and eclectic architectural styles,
while I quietly chant before a cathedral.
Rummaging through handmade beadwork
while exchanging smiles
with the friendly crowd…
I seem to have stepped on a cloud!

A sudden sway of the chilly breeze
takes me to the scent of Chinatown.

Loud rhythmical beats from a box
make the dancers' feet fly
delighting the curious passers-by.
Living statues grab the children's hearts
so they toss coins in their jars,
just like the bushman
who startles everyone from behind.

A city with flair and ambiance
in the midst of cold waters,
grapes are aged to sweeten
and lure opportunity,
its glory is as old as its story.

From a distance
someone is always watching...
alone, soundless, unmoved-
the Alcatraz,
more mysterious than the fog.

Old Friends

A window to my past,
heartbeat to my present.
They strike a chord in my song,
add vibrance to my laughter
and meaning to my tears.

Live Act

I'm seeing distant lights
in all shades of colors
at different grids of illumination,
bright in some corners
but dimmed in others.

I travel to a new place
as the pianist turns each page,
I immerse my emotions
into each world...
on one single stage!

Uncertainty

The cool air lifts my sleep
as I step on this narrow street,
a faint sound seduces me
to turn into a shadowed corner
hidden from the sun.
I can feel the steam
moistening my cheeks
as it breathes life into my wings,
telling me on the calm, to fly low
and high on its crescendo.
In the skies I meet the wind,
so I ask the earth to turn slow,
on the ground I must live
the reason for my flight.

The sound gets closer now
as the day casts a glance
at the face of its gloaming.

Behind Those Dreamy Eyes

She looks at me
with a distant gaze,
her eyes bear a smile
that is warm and familiar.
Strange laughter bursts
out of her fragile chest,
screaming soap operas
numb her constant aches.

She says,
"My hands have lost their grip."
Her cheeks are down,
her legs can find no gait.
A walker carries the weight
of someone who is laden
with so much to bear.
Years of toil,
twenty four seven,
took a toll on her…
her own narration
for family conversations
at dinners and reunions.

Her voice is gone,
her speech distorted,
she sings inside her head.
"Is there something left
to be eager for?" she asks.
I fall silent for a second.
My thoughts wander far
to her younger past…
a glimpse to my future?

Here she comes slowly
holding the walker,
its four metal legs
bearing the substance
of a woman
filled with her share
of passion and wisdom.

Behind those weary eyes
her dreams are young.

A Woman's Refuge

The wind drowns my cry
over my losses,
the passing of a chance
to laugh,
to fly,
to sing,
and even pray
at the slightest calm
of the angry sea.
I seek the time
when I could play
as sunrise bursts
to light my playground
so I could see
its endless symmetry.

Little children are laughing
while I sit in my corner.

One thought, one vision.
One life, one song.

A New Year

Again I find my feet
stepping on unfamiliar grounds,
not seeing what's ahead,
eager to find their way,
careful not to lose the balance
too elusive to many.

Turning my back
to the road behind me
that seems too far away.
Is it my eyes failing,
the sun not guiding me
or the moon shedding light
on my shadowed turns only?
I see colored images
of downturns and side turns,
unforeseen questioning of truths,
nature's offerings of
tears and exhilaration,
losses and gains.

At times glorious moments
of laughs and heavenly warmth
take me to a place
that knows no pain,
sadness,
nor disappointment.
Brevity is their trait
that makes one's spirit
desire for more .
Is it too much
for the human heart
to feel happy forever?

A refined Gregorian calendar
helps man find labels
for almost everything in life.
Unlike forever there is an end
and a beginning to everything...
but time.

Regal in Ivory

Each bead, each crystal
mirrors her moves.
They illumine her face,
adorn her figure in silken fabric
that flows fluidly as she walks.

A lone blue sapphire
dangling below her neck
rivals the ocean's depth
where lie the gems of her young life…
the winnings and losses
on unfamiliar grounds
she found outside the home
where she and I battled
the unforeseen storms.

The spirit of Pachelbel
carries us both afloat
as we process…
Her smile beams to cover
the cry in her eyes,
emotions too intense
to grab her hands away
from her dad's memory
kept alive in her bouquet.

I still see daddy's girl
in a woman full of soul,
whose eyes speak of a man
so lovingly missed
as her glance murmurs,
"Mommy, I'm ready to dance."

A Girl's Lullaby

There was a girl from San Jose,
a town quite small and sleepy.
Her face full of smiles and wonder,
her heart left open wide.

She grew up in comfort,
abundant in care.
She traveled far
to look for presents,
for them she paid the price.
As the world unfurled,
bites of mundane reality
burned her gentle heart.
The sparkle of innocence
slowly, has left her eyes.
She fought her wars
and drank her wine,
gave away gifts
to the old and young.

I hear her singing to me
a lullaby of old,
a melody of youth
waking slumbering dreams
to life.

Somewhere Is Bliss

When I soak myself
in the warmth of the sun,
let rain pour all over me
until my drenched body
turns into a shy display...
is this called bliss?

When I sail
in a quiet stream
rowing in rhythm,
dancing on a calm breeze
that I may hear
soft murmurs of the earth.
When I commune with flowers,
humble in their beauty,
their colors scream
competing for glory,
the one and only quest
for a worthy existence...
is this one bliss?

Here in this friendly home
I become a guest.
Here... is my bliss.

Fireworks

Thundering sound,
distant boom traveling louder
coming closer to my home.
You arrive in a blast,
startle me out of my haze,
my dream's gone fast.
Bursting into colors of the sun,
sparks of diamond at day,
somber in the night.
I can see you dance
to fill my vision with illusions
I try to look away
lest I forget my destiny.
This time you fly high
with the colors of emerald
spilled over from the sea,
but as I kiss the ground,
you splatter hues of blood
announcing life.
Coming out of hiding
you take one breath on me.
Again, I come alive!

This Man I Know

Fair skin smooth as a caress,
it instantly responds
to the touch of my fingertips
like it's one with mine.
Brown hair, brown eyes,
teasing eyelashes,
a delightful sight.
A face grown too familiar
whose lines I can see
with my closed eyes.
A jolt of strength, fiery desire
spreading nowhere but here
in the midst of our hearts.
Playful, warm affection,
at times too intense
to calm the wind blowing
through the windows of our home.

A mouth that made me taste
the kiss that lingers
long after the wine has dried
the softest edges of my lips.
Hands that serve me my daily bread,
fragrant spices, exotic herbs.
Smile that sings to me lullabies
so I can drift off to a dreamy night.
Arms that wrap my body
when shivers run through my chest.
Eyes that drink with me
the crimson hues
from the rarest sunsets.

A voice that so often calls my name
with a million different sounds.
He takes the moon out of the sky
so I can play with its light
when darkness dims my earth.
A heart that easily tears
when I feel pain,
when nature plays
with my human strength.
He offers countless little things,
I store them all in a treasure box
for my future memory
that only the young
would remember.

Ancient Thread

Threads delicately stained
with colors of the earth,
intricate designs of seduction
splashed over fabrics,
that would soon age in time.
Cotton, silk, and satin,
gifts from grains and worms,
sometimes you're tinted in red
pulsating with excitement ,
flowing like the invisible wind.
What have you seen so far,
where have you been?
Always covering, protecting
beauties in hiding,
offering a lifestyle of elegance
only in brief, glorious moments
that would soon blink away.
Service done, short life span,
you're thrown into a pile
abandoned in a closet,
out of the way and forgotten
destined to fray and decay.

Every strand interwoven
into many lives of vanity.
Once a living witness
to every woman's glory,
her endless love stories,
too long for a storyteller,
too short for a hungry lover.

When Truth Becomes Silent

What if a smile is not a smile
but a mere veil of sadness
that has grown
through years of grief?
What if a smile is only used
to draw hearts near
a crying child?
Fear can lose its power
in a borrowed time
but can return later
to collect a mounting debt.
Like a branch of a tree
beaten by heat and rain,
it can snap from the trunk,
or choose to grow a new leaf.

Truth has been silent too long,
let me live to find its voice.

Butterflies

Well kept secrets in a quiet cocoon
slowly transform you into flying colors,
brilliant, magical, and beautiful!
Golden, black, blue,
yellow, brown, and crimson,
lines, spots, and dots.
Intricate patterns designed on wings
flapping hurriedly to catch a chance in life.
Specks of pollen spread on a million tiny buds
as a call of duty, a messenger
from the goddess of beauty.
You patiently wait in hiding
to see the sun,
then soar with the wind!
Share with me the gift from your goddess.
Teach me patience.
Passion.
Love.

From Here to There

I am here sipping the air
to fill my heart and limbs,
tackling the daily tasks
learned from my teachers,
a necessary cycle of existence.

I entered a world of strangers
whose language I don't speak,
smiles I don't wear.
They cover their faces
with masks of different shapes
and tell me stories
with unfinished endings .
There at a distance,
I see sunrays peeking through
the holes in the clouds,
streaming along the valley,
where in total abandon
the children play.
Everyone there speaks words
with the sweetest sounds.
The music they sing
are written in the skies
with lyrics of unspoken beauty
touching ancient souls.
I start a few steps
toward this destined place
but the climbs are rough,
ravines are deep,
woods thick and darkened,
typhoons unforeseen.
If the heavens spare
a silver streak of dawn
its light will see me through
dark passages unknown.

As soon as I arrive there
more treasures will unravel
then I will see who I am, again.

I spend a lifetime here
but always know-
home is waiting there.

Slow Ride to Destiny

Time is fast when I run,
slow when I seek what I desire
to shape my fate.
But where is time when I need it most?
It's become elusive as I count the years.
I start racing against it,
not walking with it.
If time has rhythm I wish to find it
so I may dance and flow in its river.
The river is calm when it's deep,
noisy and rough
when running on a rocky path.
The ride is slow to where I'm going,
time is not enough.
Could it be that time does not exist
when measured on my terms?
Perhaps time is an illusion
when my soul yearns
for the soft velvet of a kiss,
the cool droplets of mist
moistening my lips
when my spirit thirsts
for a sip of peace.

I long to travel deep and far…
and if time becomes my friend,
I'll take but one, slow ride.

Stained Glass Windows

My eyes are drawn to your colors
enriched by stories told and untold.
Behind the shut windows
are countless rituals
begging for blessings
for us to learn origins of beings.
Stored inside, concealed by your lights
are sins and lessons learned,
mysteries of old held in faith,
never understood by men.
Lives and deaths come and go
the cycle does not end.
Is heaven a fulfillment?

I kiss the earth and live to love,
"Come here and now!"
I beg my heaven aloud.

Sol

Sometimes I wonder
how she came to choose me
or did I choose her?
Sweet woman,
she is the breeze that whispers
through the open sea.
She is the rain feeding
the leaves of the acacia tree,
generous with her shade,
protective of the needy .
Brave as a bird soaring high,
flying away from clouds
that are gray and hanging low.
The sun gives her strength,
warmth that bears her name.
Soothing voice,
sound of the divine
a gift for the blind
who has ears for the eternal.
I was blind before but deaf no longer
because of her presence,
a mystery within my genes .

I am a child of a sound
ever longing to be heard,
I weave words and sing music
to bring eternity near.
I write songs with no endings,
I am my mother's daughter.

Shy Moon

A glimmer of light hesitant to shine,
hiding behind clouds, flying low
to smell the scented waters
playing beneath my feet.
I only see the promising edges,
clouds looking like petals
trimmed with dust of gold.
It peeks wanting to know
if I find the fluid staircase
on the ocean's floor.
Its rays break into pieces
like a million diamonds
scattered and glittering,
luring my body to move in.
You must know my secret desires,
you must hear my innermost voice
from the old, forgotten generation.
Do you ever get tired
giving hope to dreamers
when you roam in the sky
with your borrowed light?
You follow my every move
even when you shy away.

If inspiration links my day to the next
your beauty holds each breath I take .

Lucas Gabriel

No Tears to Shed

My eyes are dry as pain travels
through my consciousness,
I seek relief but find none.
My scream inside grows
louder than thunder
yet bears a muted voice,
tears want to flow
but find no path in my eyes.
I lost the face of joy
when I tried to grab it
by looking into a mirror
that had no reflection
but distance and loneliness
spilling over my dominion.

Sands

You are a soft bed under my feet.
I walk lazily, slowly,
so I can delay your wings
from soaring in the air
to race against my steps.
What have I done to lose my grip
on your elusive tail?
I'm always running behind,
it seems so nowadays.
Sands in a bottle,
don't fall to the bottom.
Tell me I'm not late
chasing dreams that never rest.
When the sun blinds my eyes
and its heat paints a blur
I need to learn to see
with my own heart.
You're as vast as the ocean
and the neighboring shores
yet too fine for my hands.
You design a way
to escape through my fingers
each time I hold your grains.

The stars are still flickering
somewhere in a distant space.
Let not my eyes be fooled
by their traveling light,
as only time can tell
which glow is real.

Sound of Laughter

Where are you in this empty stare?
Are you somewhere deep
in your travel?
Do you see the light shining near,
are you feeling pain again?
Is it love that's hurting
or the search for the touch
that has eluded you?
Do you cry inside and hide,
do you smile at my follies,
this girl standing on your footsteps,
the voice that was once your child?
I see your face move
resembling the olden sun.
I still hear the crisp trill,
the excited wave
mounting on the wind,
soft at times,
loud now,
loud as your laughter...
whose sound is no longer there.

Voice of a Poet

It was always there
in the deepest rift of my veins
thriving unseen.
It grew into a heart
beating endlessly,
nagging restlessly
to make a sound,
not of the common kind
but of the divine.
I hum and sing to imitate the birds,
the sound of the whistling wind,
the violent rage of the storm,
the quiet whispers of the grass.
Music is the language
of my dreams, my desires.
I breathe in what I see,
bring life into what I hear.
The voice tells me
to ride every sunset,
dance with ocean waves,
bloom to seduce a night
when passion chooses life.
I string words to open doors
to the world of beauty
lest it remains in obscurity.
I meditate with notes and symbols
to connect with old souls.
I listen to the voice,
it listens to me.
The voice was there before I was born
with my mind captive in eternity.

CPSIA information can be obtained at www.ICGtesting.com
Printed in the USA
LVOW10s0000260515

439827LV00001B/9/P